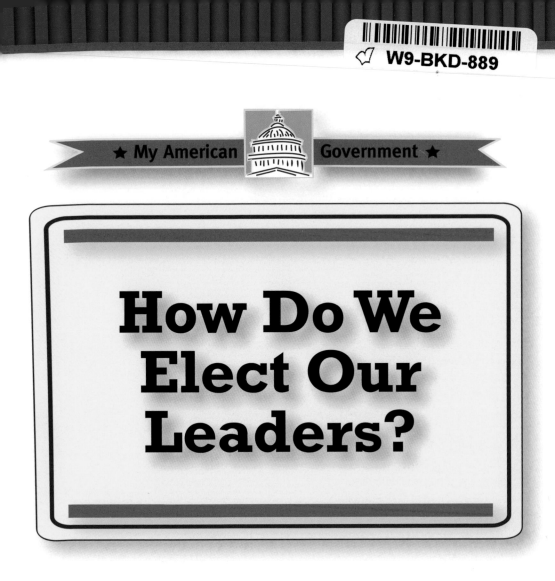

★ My American Government ★

How Do We Elect Our Leaders?

By William David Thomas

Gareth Stevens
Publishing

Please visit our web site at www.garethstevens.com. For a free catalog describing Gareth Stevens Publishing's list of high-quality books, call 1-800-542-2595 (USA) or 1-800-387-3178 (Canada). Gareth Stevens Publishing's fax: 1-877-542-2596

Library of Congress Cataloging-in-Publication Data

Thomas, William, 1947-
    How do we elect our leaders? / William David Thomas.
        p. cm.—(My American government)
    Includes bibliographical references and index.
    ISBN-10: 0-8368-8860-X   ISBN-13: 978-0-8368-8860-7 (lib. bdg.: alk. paper)
    ISBN-10: 0-8368-8865-0   ISBN-13: 978-0-8368-8865-2 (softcover: alk. paper)
    1. Elections—United States—Juvenile literature. 2. United States—Politics and Government—Juvenile literature. I. Title.
    JK1978T56   2008
    324.60973—dc22   2007028173

This edition first published in 2008 by
Gareth Stevens Publishing
A Weekly Reader® Company
1 Reader's Digest Road
Pleasantville, NY 10570-7000 USA

Senior Managing Editor: Lisa M. Guidone
Creative Director: Lisa Donovan
Cover Designer: Jeannie Friedman
Interior Designer: Yin Ling Wong
Photo Researchers: Kimberly Babbitt and Charlene Pinckney

Picture Credits: Cover, title page: Jupiter Images; p. 5 © Rick Freidman/Corbis; p. 7 Shutterstock; p. 8 Charles Krupa/AP; p. 9 Victoria Arocho/AP; p. 10 © Corbis; p. 11 © Hulton-Deutsch Collection/Corbis; p. 13 © Gareth Stevens; p.15 © Wally McNamee/Corbis; p. 17 © Reuters/Corbis; p. 19 Timothy A. Clary/AFP/Getty Images; p. 20 Susan Walsh/AP; p. 22 Bob Daemmrich/Corbis; p. 23 Courtesy of Governor Rick Perry's office; p. 24 Tim Sloan/AFP/Getty Images; p. 26 © David Saffran/Icon SMI/Corbis; p. 28 Luis Martinez/AP; p. 29 J. Pat Carter/AP

Printed in the United States of America

 2 3 4 5 6 7 8 9 10 09 08

Contents

Words in the glossary appear in **bold** type the first time they are used in the text.

CHAPTER 1

★

A Cup of Coffee

It happened in a small town in New Hampshire. It was a cold winter morning in 1980. Martha was working the breakfast shift in her coffee shop. Her regular customers were arriving. They sat at the counter or at their usual tables. Martha went around the room, pouring coffee and taking orders for eggs, toast, and pancakes.

A stranger came in and went to one of the tables. He shook hands with the folks sitting there, talked to them for a few minutes, and then moved on to another table. When Martha brought their breakfast orders, she brought a cup of coffee for the stranger, too.

A few minutes later two men from the local newspaper showed up. They talked to the stranger and took his picture. After speaking with most of the people in the coffee shop, the stranger left. He waved as he walked out the door.

Martha picked up some of the dirty dishes. She asked one of her customers, "Who was that guy?"

"Are you kidding?"

"No, I'm not kidding. Who was he?"

"Martha, that was Ronald Reagan."

"Ronald Reagan, the man who used to be an actor?"

"Yes."

"What's he doing here?"

Ronald Reagan speaks to a crowd in Concord, New Hampshire, in 1980. Reagan (shown here with his wife, Nancy) won the state's primary election.

"He's running for president."

"Of what?"

"Of the United States!"

"Well, he's sure not getting my vote."

"Why not?"

"He didn't pay for his coffee!"

Some people say that's a true story, and some say it's not. But it could be true. Every four years, people who want to be president head to New Hampshire. That state traditionally holds the country's first presidential **primary election**.

Presidential hopefuls travel around the state. They visit coffee shops, dairy farms, colleges, shoe stores, and factories. They make speeches and listen to people. They shake lots of hands and even kiss a baby or two. And sometimes, they forget to pay for their coffee. It's all part of how we Americans elect our leaders.

★

CHAPTER 2

Electing the President

In the United States, the presidential election is held every four years. People who want to be president have to start work early. They often begin their **campaigns** two years before the election. Running for president takes a lot of time. It also takes a lot of money. Some of that money comes from the major **political parties**.

WHO CAN BE PRESIDENT?

The **U.S. Constitution** lists three requirements to be president. A person must:

- be a U.S. citizen at birth (a natural-born citizen).
- have lived in the United States for the last fourteen years.
- be at least thirty-five years old.

Political Parties

A political party is a group of people who have the same ideas about laws and government. There are two main political parties in the United States: the Republican Party and the Democratic Party. There are many smaller parties, too. All political parties work to get their **candidates** elected. Members give money to the party. They also write letters, make signs, and go to meetings.

PARTY ANIMALS!

Democrat Andrew Jackson ran for president in 1828. His opponents called him a donkey. Jackson put pictures of donkeys on his campaign posters. Democrats have been doing it ever since. In 1874, the political cartoonist Thomas Nast drew a picture for a weekly publication. It showed a donkey dressed in a lion costume, scaring other animals. A frightened elephant in the cartoon was labeled "Republican Vote." From then on, the elephant has been the symbol of the Republican Party.

Primaries and Caucuses

Often, several people want to be a party's candidate for president. Primary elections help the party decide which person to support. Each of the big parties holds its own primary elections in separate states. In many states, only people who are members of a party can vote in the primary election.

The primaries usually begin very early in an election year. The first one has traditionally taken place in New Hampshire. Instead of a primary, some states hold a **caucus**. In a caucus, members of a political party hold a meeting to choose their candidate for president. Iowa usually holds the first caucus. Primaries and caucuses continue through the first part of the year.

Voters are often polled during the primaries. Polling companies telephone them to ask questions, such as "Which candidate do you think will do more to help schools?" The poll results may appear on television, in newspapers, or in advertising.

JOIN THE PARTY!

There are lots of political parties in the U.S. The Green Party supports clean air, land, and water. The Labor Party supports workers rights and pay. The Libertarian Party wants less government and lower taxes.

In June 2007, these eight Democrats were seeking their party's presidential nomination. They met for a **debate** in Manchester, New Hampshire.

Posters, banners, and cheering are all part of national conventions, where each party officially announces its candidate for president.

The Conventions

After the primaries and caucuses, each major party chooses its candidate at a **national convention**. The conventions are big, exciting shows. They are held during the summer before Election Day. Party leaders share their ideas on major issues, such as education or health care. **Delegates** from each state cast votes. The party's **nomination** goes to the candidate with the most votes. Once a presidential candidate is chosen, he or she names someone to run as vice president. When the two big party conventions are over, the election contest really begins.

Campaigning

Before and after the conventions, the presidential candidates travel across the country. They meet people and give speeches. They use television and radio advertising, mailings, and web sites to persuade people to vote for them. Movie stars, athletes, and singers may speak in support of a candidate.

The candidates also take part in televised debates. There may be two or three of these during an election campaign. The candidates appear on the same stage. They answer questions about important issues and talk about their plans for the country.

Senator John F. Kennedy (left) debates Vice President Richard Nixon (right). Both ran for president in 1960. This election marked the first time debates between presidential candidates were shown on television.

Money plays a very important role in all of this. Presidential campaigns can cost more than $100 million. Candidates and their parties spend a lot of time and effort raising money.

Presidential candidate Franklin D. Roosevelt shakes hands with a farmer in Georgia in 1932. Later that year, Roosevelt was elected president for the first time.

ONE, TWO (NOT THREE) TERMS AND YOU'RE OUT

The U.S. Constitution said the president would serve a term of four years. It did not say originally how many terms a president could serve. For 150 years, no one served more than two terms. Franklin D. Roosevelt was elected in 1932, and re-elected in 1936. In 1940, Roosevelt was elected for a third term. In 1944, Roosevelt was elected to a fourth term. He died in office less than a year later. In 1951, an **amendment** was added to the U.S. Constitution. The Twenty-Second Amendment limits the president to two terms.

Election Day

All the campaigning leads up to Election Day. The presidential election is always held the first Tuesday after the first Monday in November. When Americans cast their vote on Election Day, it is called the **popular vote**. But they're not voting directly for a candidate. They're voting for a group of electors who pledge to support the candidate that wins the popular vote.

The Electoral College

The electors in each state actually vote for the president. The group of electors make up the **Electoral College**. Each elector is chosen by political parties in each state. Each state gets a certain number of electors. The number is equal to the state's total members of Congress (senators plus representatives). States with more people have more electoral votes. California gets fifty-five electoral votes. Ohio gets twenty. Vermont gets only three. Although it is not a state, Washington, D.C., gets three electoral votes.

Electors cast their votes in December—a few weeks after Election Day. They usually meet in the capital city of their state. In most cases, the candidate who wins the most popular votes in a state gets all of that state's electoral votes.

All together, there are 538 electoral votes. To win the election, a candidate must get 270 of them. If no candidate gets that many, the House of Representatives votes to choose the president. This has happened twice, in 1800 and 1824.

THE ELECTORAL COLLEGE

The numbers on the map show the 2008 electoral votes for each state.

Note: Alaska and Hawaii are not drawn to scale and are not placed in their geographic locations.

STAY OR GO?

The Electoral College is part of the U.S. Constitution. To change it would require a constitutional amendment. That would be a long and difficult process. But is the Electoral College a good idea? Some people think the United States should get rid of the Electoral College because it is unfair. One reason is that a candidate can get the most votes from the people, but not become president. This happened in 1876, 1888, and 2000. Other people argue that we should keep the Electoral College. They say the system has worked since George Washington was elected president more than 200 years ago.

Inauguration Day

The president officially begins the new term on **Inauguration Day**. January 20th is Inauguration Day. On this day, the president takes the **Oath of Office**. The Oath of Office is the president's pledge to lead the country and follow the rules of the U.S. Constitution. The president recites the same oath that was taken by George Washington in 1789—and every president since then.

INAUGURATION FIRSTS

- George Washington's first inauguration in 1789 took place at Federal Hall in New York City, which was then the country's capital. Washington's second inaugural speech, in 1793, was the shortest on record. At only 135 words, it lasted just eight minutes. The inauguration took place in Philadelphia.
- In 1841, William Henry Harrison gave the longest inaugural address. At 8,445 words, it lasted almost two hours!
- In 1925, Calvin Coolidge's inaugural speech was the first broadcast on the radio.
- In 1937, Franklin D. Roosevelt became the first president to be inaugurated on January 20, the date required by the Twentieth Amendment to the U.S. Constitution. Prior to that, the inauguration was on March 4.
- Harry S. Truman's speech in 1949 was the first to be shown on television.
- In 1997, Bill Clinton's inauguration was the first to be transmitted over the Internet.

The Capitol in Washington, D.C. is covered with flags and banners for the first inauguration of George W. Bush on January 20, 2001.

THE ELECTION OF 2000

The presidential election of 2000 was one of the most **controversial** in American history. Vice President Al Gore ran against Texas Governor George W. Bush. More people voted for Gore than Bush, but the votes in the Electoral College were very close. It became clear that whoever got Florida's electoral votes would win. But there was trouble with voting **ballots** in Florida. Votes were counted and then counted again. Lawyers and courts got into the counting. The case went to the Supreme Court—the top court in the United States. The Court ruled that the counting had to stop. Bush was declared the winner in Florida by a little more than 500 votes. He got the state's electoral votes and won the election.

★

CHAPTER 3

Electing Members of Congress

Writing the U.S. Constitution was not an easy job. There were a lot of discussions. Many of them were about Congress, the law-making branch of the U.S. government. Should states with more people have more lawmakers? Should all states have the same number? The final agreement was a plan called the Great Compromise. It said that Congress would have two houses, or groups of lawmakers: the Senate and the House of Representatives. In the House of Representatives, states with more people would have more representatives. In the Senate, each state would have two senators.

★ ★ ★ ★ ★ ★ ★ ★ ★ ★ ★ ★ ★ ★ ★ ★ ★ ★ ★

WHO CAN BE A MEMBER OF CONGRESS?

To be elected to the House of Representatives, you must:	To be elected to the Senate, you must:
• be at least 25 years old. • have been a citizen of the U.S. for seven years. • live in the state you want to represent.	• be at least 30 years old. • have been a citizen of the U.S. for nine years. • live in the state you want to represent.

In March 2007, the King of Jordan delivered a speech to both houses of Congress at the U.S. Capitol in Washington, D.C.

Electing Senators

For many years, senators were not elected by the people. They were chosen by the state **legislatures**. This process changed in 1913. The Seventeenth Amendment to the Constitution said that senators must be elected by a direct vote of the people in their state.

Today, there are one hundred U.S. senators—two from each state. Every two years, one-third of them are up for re-election. Senators are elected to serve a six-year term. There is no limit to how many terms a senator can serve.

The biggest political parties in each state—the Republicans and Democrats—decide who will run for the Senate. If a party has several candidates, it may hold a primary election. This helps the party decide which candidate has the best chance to win.

Not all candidates for the Senate come from the big parties, however. Independent candidates and those from small political parties can run as well. They have to meet state requirements to be on the election ballot. For example, they may have to submit a petition signed by a certain number of registered voters.

Senate elections are always held on the first Tuesday after the first Monday in November. They take place in even number years: 2008, 2010, and so on. In most states, whoever gets the most votes wins.

PARTY POWER

You may have heard about the majority party in Congress. A political party has a majority when its members hold more than half of the seats. One party may have the majority in the House or the Senate—or both! That gives the party a lot of power. The majority party may have enough votes to pass or stop a law. The majority party also picks leaders of important committees. These committees often decide how bills are written and which ones are voted on to become laws. In every election, the two main political parties try to win more seats so they can remain or become the majority party in Congress.

In 2000, former First Lady Hillary Rodham Clinton was elected to the U.S. Senate from New York.

Electing Representatives

Although every state has two senators, they have different numbers of representatives in Congress. The exact number of representatives depends on the state's population. States with more people, such as California, have more representatives than states with fewer people, such as Vermont.

Each state is divided into congressional districts. Each district gets one representative. There must be about the same number of people living in each district. Of course, this means that districts are different sizes. The whole state of Wyoming is just one congressional district. People in the city of Chicago are divided among several districts.

Members of the House represent only the people in their district. This means that representatives can more easily get to know the needs of those people. They can better serve those people and the communities where they live.

Representative Nancy Pelosi of California is surrounded by the children and grandchildren of other members of Congress. She celebrates after becoming the first woman ever elected Speaker of the House, in January 2007.

THE GERRYMANDER

There are 435 congressional districts in the United States. Each one must have about the same number of people. But the population of districts keeps changing. As a result, congressional districts must be re-drawn from time to time. Politicians try to draw districts in ways that will help more of their party's candidates get elected. This is called gerrymandering. The word comes from a man's name. Elbridge Gerry was once governor of Massachusetts. While he was in office, some really strange election districts were drawn. One of them was shaped like a salamander. A newspaper man said it should be called a gerrymander.

As with Senate elections, political parties decide who will run for the House. If a party has several candidates, there may be a primary election. The winner will be the party's candidate for his or her district. Independent candidates and those from small political parties can run as well.

Members of the House serve two-year terms. There is no limit to how many times they can run for re-election. House elections are held in even-numbered years. They are always held on the first Tuesday after the first Monday in November.

COUNTING PEOPLE IN PLACES

The number of representatives from a state can increase or decrease. It depends on the state's population. But the population of the country—and each state—keeps changing. So every ten years, the U.S. government counts the people. This is called the census. It is required by the U.S. Constitution. Today, some of the counting is done with forms sent through the mail. Some of it, however, is still done by census workers who go from door to door.

A census worker interviews a homeowner in Texas during the 2000 census. Questions include the names and ages of people living in a house, how long they have lived there, the number of bedrooms and bathrooms, and much more.

★

CHAPTER 4

Electing State Officials

Like the U.S. government, states have elected officials. As in national elections, the big political parties choose candidates to run for state offices. If there are several candidates, a party may hold a primary election. Independent and small-party candidates may run, too. They must meet state requirements to get on the ballot. Most state elections take place in November. What officials are elected? What are they called? How long do they serve? The answers are different in each state.

In April 2007, tornadoes destroyed homes and businesses in Texas. Governor Rick Perry—at the microphones—told people how the state would help them.

Governors

Every state has a governor. He or she is the highest official in a state. Each state decides the requirements for being governor. These may include age, place of birth, and how long the person

PRESIDENTIAL TRAINING

Often state governors go on to become president of the United States. Since 1976, four governors have been elected president. Jimmy Carter was governor of Georgia. Ronald Reagan was governor of California. Bill Clinton was governor of Arkansas, and George W. Bush was governor of Texas.

These former governors—George W. Bush (left), Bill Clinton (center), and Jimmy Carter (right)—all went on to become president of the United States.

has lived in the state. States also decide how long a governor serves. In New Hampshire and Vermont, the governor serves a two-year term. But in most other states, the governor serves for four years. Many states limit their governors to two terms. Utah allows its governor to serve up to twelve years.

State Legislatures

There are lots of differences among state legislatures, starting with size. New Hampshire is a small state, but it has the biggest state legislature. Four hundred twenty-four lawmakers work there! The next largest state legislature is in Pennsylvania. It has two hundred fifty members. Wyoming has just ninety.

Most state legislatures have two houses. One house is usually called the House of Representatives or the Assembly. Members represent only a certain district within their states. Only people living in that district can vote for them. The other house is always called the Senate. In states with small populations, senators represent everyone. People across the state can vote for them. In larger states, senators represent a specific district, and only its residents may vote for them.

YOU GO, GIRL!

Women in Wyoming got the right to vote in 1869—more than fifty years before women in many other states. And in 1925, Wyoming became the first state to elect a woman governor, Nellie Tayloe Ross.

Each state decides how long a term of office lasts. In Maine, state senators and representatives serve two-year terms. In Arkansas, California, and New York, state assembly members also serve two-year terms. State senators in those states serve four-year terms.

Most states also set limits on how many terms can be served. In Ohio and Colorado, assembly members are limited to four terms. State senators are limited to two terms. In Oklahoma, house members can serve for six terms. State senators can serve three terms.

Local Governments

County, city, and town governments have their own rules about electing officials. Mayors, judges, sheriffs, and school board members may be elected. Local governments hold elections in ways that work best for the people in the area.

In 2006, New York City Mayor Michael Bloomberg (right) shoveled up some dirt to start building a new baseball stadium for the Mets. He was helped by ballplayers Jose Reyes (left) and David Wright (center).

★

CHAPTER 5

The Importance of Voting

Try to imagine this. In a certain country, there was a large group of people who had a legal right to vote. But another group of people would not let them. When they tried to vote, they were arrested. Their homes were burned. Some of them were killed.

All of this really happened, right here in the United States, less than sixty years ago. Those people were African Americans. It took years of hardship and courage, but their right to vote was finally upheld.

The Right To Vote

Americans live in a **representative democracy.** It is a form of government that gives people the power to elect their leaders. Americans vote for people to represent them and make decisions. Voting is the most important right Americans have. There are many places in the world where people do not have the right to vote. They can't choose their leaders. They have no voice in the government. Voting is a right that Americans have died for. And sadly, it is a right that many Americans ignore.

EVERY VOTE COUNTS

One of the closest elections in U.S. history took place in 2004. Christine Gregoire was elected governor of the state of Washington. The votes for the whole state were counted three times. Gregoire won by a grand total of just 129 votes!

One of the biggest political problems in the United States today is that people just don't vote. In the 2000 election, only half of the people in the United States voted. People who don't vote give up their chance to make a difference!

VOTING DOWN UNDER

In Australia, 95 percent of the people vote in elections. They have to. It's the law! Voting is required in Australia. People who don't vote can be fined. They may even go to jail.

This bus was part of the "Rock The Vote" presidential campaign in 2004. The campaign put together speeches, rock music, and singers to encourage young people to vote. ▼

Citizens often wait in line to cast their votes.

Who Can Vote?

Are you are a citizen of the United States? If so, when you are eighteen years old, you can register to vote. You will then have the right to vote in local, state, and national elections. You can vote for the president of the United States. You can help choose the governor of your state. You can vote on whether to buy new computers for your school district. No matter what the issue, voting gives you a say in how things are done.

WHO WANTS TO BE A MILLIONAIRE?

A man in Arizona wants more people to vote. He is trying to get a new law passed. The law would give people a lottery ticket if they vote. One voter could win a million dollars.

Glossary

amendment: an official change to the U.S. Constitution

ballot: a printed or electronic form used for voting

campaign: a series of actions that are planned and done to reach a goal

candidate: a person who is running for office

caucus: a special meeting in which members of a political party choose their candidate for president

controversial: something that causes people to take sides or argue

debate: a formal discussion between people or groups who disagree

delegate: a person who represents others

Electoral College: the group of 538 people who officially elect the U.S. president

Inauguration Day: the ceremonies, including the Oath of Office, that mark the start of a president's term

legislature: the law-making body in a government

national convention: a large gathering at which a political party officially announces its candidate for president

nomination: naming someone to run for office

Oath of Office: the pledge that the U.S. president takes to follow the rules set forth in the U.S. Constitution

political party: a group of people who have similar ideas about the government and laws

popular vote: the number of votes cast on Election Day

primary election: a state election in which political party members vote for their candidate for president

representative democracy: a form of government in which people vote to elect the country's leaders

U.S. Constitution: the written plan and laws of the U.S. government

To Find Out More

Books

America Votes: How Our President Is Elected. Linda Granfield. (Kids Can Press)

Congress. Watts Library: U.S. Government & Military (series). Suzanne LeVert. (Scholastic Library Publishing)

Constitution Translated for Kids. Cathy Travis (Synergy Books)

Our Elections. I Know America (series). Richard Steins. (The Millbrook Press)

Web Sites

The Democracy Project
www.pbskids.org/democracy/vote/index.html

Ben Franklin's Guide to the U.S. Government
bensguide.gpo.gov/3-5/election/index.html

Kids in the House: the Office of the Clerk of the House of Representatives
www.clerkkids.house.gov

Kids Voting
www.kidsvotingusa.org/page9597.cfm

Publisher's note to educators and parents: Our editors have carefully reviewed these web sites to ensure that they are suitable for children. Many web sites change frequently, however, and we cannot guarantee that a site's future contents will continue to meet our high standards of quality and educational value. Be advised that children should be closely supervised whenever they access the Internet.

Index

About the Author

William David Thomas lives in Rochester, New York, where he works with students who have special needs. Bill has written software documentation, advertising copy, children's books, magazine articles, an occasional poem, and lots of letters. Bill claims he was once King of Fiji, but gave up the throne to pursue a career as a relief pitcher. It's not true.